# Japan

## *Clare Boast*

Heinemann Interactive Library
Des Plaines, Illinois

Published by Heinemann Interactive Library,
an imprint of Reed Educational & Professional Publishing,
1350 East Touhy Avenue, Suit 240 West, Des Plaines, IL 60018

Produced by Times Offset (M) Sdn. Bhd.
Designed by AMR
Illustrations by Art Construction

02 01 00 99 98
10 9 8 7 6 5 4 3 2 1

Boast, Clare, 1965–
    Japan / Clare Boast
        p.   cm. – – (Next stop!)
    Includes bibliographical references and index.
    Summary: An introduction to the history, geography, culture, and modern daily life in Japan.
    ISBN 1-57572-568-1 (library binding)
    1. Japan – – Juvenile literature.   [1. Japan.]   I. Title.
II. Series.                                                           97-19805
DS806.B53 1997                                                       C I P
952 – – DC21                                                          AC

**Acknowledgments**
The author and publisher are grateful to the following for permission to reproduce copyright photographs: J Allan Cash Ltd, pp.10, 19, 24; Colorific! H. Aga p.25, B. Martin p.8, H. Sautter p.23; Robert Harding Picture Library Ltd p.29; Trip: Trip pp.12, 13, 14, 16, 17, 21, Art Directors p.26, J. Dakers p.6, J. Holmes p.15, T. Morse pp.27–28, P. Rauter pp.18, 22, C. Rennie pp.4, 5, 9, 11, A. Tovy pp.6, 22.

Cover photograph reproduced with permission of:
    background: Tony Stone Images, Yann Layma.
    child: Image Bank, Stephen Marks.

Special thanks to Betty Root for her comments in the preparation of this book.

Every effort has been made to contact copyright holders of any material reproduced in this book. Any omissions will be rectified in subsequent printings if notice is given to the publisher.

Words in the book in bold, **like this**, are explained in the glossary on page 31.

# CONTENTS

# INTRODUCTION

## WHERE IS JAPAN?

Japan is made up of more than 4,000 **islands**. These islands stretch out in a line in the Pacific Ocean. Most of the 125 million people live on the four biggest islands: Hokkaido, Honshu, Shikoku, and Kyushu.

**Hiroshima was bombed in 1945. This building was left unrepaired as a reminder of the people who died.**

CHINA

RUSSIA

NORTH KOREA

SOUTH KOREA

Sapporo

*Hokkaido*

0  120 miles

Sendai

Niigata

*Honshu*

TOKYO

Kyoto    Kawasaki
         Yokohama
Kobe    Nagoya

Hiroshima

Osaka

J A P A N

Fukuoka

Nagasaki

*Shikoku*

Kagoshima

*Kyushu*

SOUTH KOREA

120 miles

*Kyushu*

CHINA

*Ryukyu Islands*

TAIWAN

**City Population**

○  over 1,000,000

●  over 100,000

●  capital

# JAPAN'S HISTORY

At first, Japan was ruled by warriors, then **emperors**. These rulers did not want to have anything to do with other countries. But by 100 years ago, Japan was trading with other countries. It then fought in World War II, which ended in 1945 when the first **atomic bomb** was dropped on Hiroshima.

Today, Japan is a peaceful country. It is also very rich. Japan makes a lot of **goods**, especially electronic goods, to sell all over the world.

*Japan means "land of the rising sun".*

**The Golden Pavilion in Kyoto, on Honshu, was built in 1397. It is a temple for one of the religions of Japan, Buddhism.**

5

# THE LAND

Japan has had many earthquakes. These homes in Kobe were hit by an earthquake in 1995.

## MOUNTAINS AND VALLEYS

Most of Japan is covered with steep mountains. The streams and rivers that run down from these mountains to the sea have made deep valleys. The rivers usually flood in the rainy season, or when the snow melts on the mountains in the summer.

This mountain is called Mount Fuji. It is a volcano, but it has not erupted for many years.

## PLAINS

Some of the land is flat. These flat plains are at the bottom of the valleys and along the **coast**.

# VOLCANOES

Many of Japan's mountains are **volcanoes**. They can erupt, throwing out ash and rocks, which rain down on places nearby. Volcanoes also pour out **lava** that flows down the mountains, burning everything in its way.

# EARTHQUAKES

Japan also has earthquakes, which make the ground shake. Earthquakes can be small, but big earthquakes can destroy buildings and roads, and kill many people.

*Japan can have up to three small earthquakes every day. Buildings are built to move with these small earthquakes.*

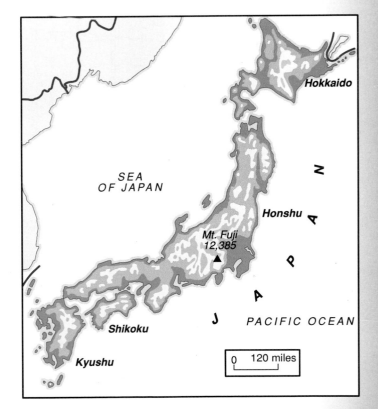

0 120 miles

Kyushu

EAST
CHINA
SEA

Ryukyu Islands

PACIFIC
OCEAN

**Height in feet**
over 3,000
1,500–3,000
600–1,500
0–600

Hokkaido

SEA
OF JAPAN

Honshu

Mt. Fuji
12,385

Shikoku

Kyushu

PACIFIC OCEAN

N

J A P A N

0    120 miles

# WEATHER, PLANTS, AND ANIMALS

## THE WEATHER

The north and south of Japan are far apart, so the weather is very different.

The north is colder than the south and has lots of snow. In the south, it is warm all year round.

Most of Japan has a "rainy season" between June and September. It rains hard almost every day. In September there are often strong winds called **typhoons**.

**Very few people go outside in the rainy season in Japan without an umbrella!**

Tourists go up Mount Fuji by cable car. Trees cover the parts of the mountains that are too steep to farm.

## PLANTS AND ANIMALS

The plants in Japan change from north to the south. They change as you go higher up, too. In the south there are plants and trees that like hot, wet weather. They could not grow in the north. There are fir trees in the mountains, but oak and maple trees grow lower down. The flat land has been cleared for farming and industry.

There are many wild animals in Japan. You can find monkeys, bears, foxes, and poisonous snakes.

*In Japan, there is a sort of lizard (a type of salamander) that grows up to 5 feet long.*

# TOWNS AND CITIES

**A busy street in Tokyo. The bridge is for trains that run above the streets.**

## TOKYO

Tokyo is the **capital city** of Japan. About 12 million people live there. It is a modern city with universities, theaters, museums, libraries, offices, and stores.

Most of old Tokyo was destroyed by an earthquake in 1923. It was rebuilt, but was destroyed again by bombing during World War 11. After this, Tokyo's buildings were rebuilt to move with earthquakes, so they would not fall down.

## OTHER TOWNS AND CITIES

All of Japan's cities and towns are very crowded. Many of them are built on the narrow, flat plains between the high mountains and the sea. There is not much space for cities and towns to grow, and many people want to live there. Homes are usually small.

## MAKING MORE SPACE

Some cities are so crowded that they have filled the sea with rocks and built on this land. Osaka's airport is built out into the sea.

*People built tall buildings to save space. Some cities make builders pay a "sunshine tax" if new buildings block out the sun from existing buildings.*

**Nagasaki is squeezed in between the mountains and the sea. About 450,000 people live there.**

# LIVING IN TOKYO

The family lives in a house on the edge of Tokyo. It has five rooms but there is no yard.

## THE SHISHIDO FAMILY

Hajime and Junko Shishido live in Tokyo. They have one girl, Emi, who is thirteen, and one boy, Yuta, who is ten. The children's grandparents, Tadao and Fumi, live there, too. In Japan, most grandparents live with the family.

## THE FAMILY'S DAY

Hajime and Junko work all week. Junko finishes at 2:00 P.M., but Hajime often works until 9:00 P.M. The children go to school, while their grandparents stay home and help with the housework.

The family can eat their evening meal together on weekends.

Yuta goes to school at 7:00 A.M. He comes back at 3:00 P.M.

## MEALTIMES

Junko does most of her food shopping in the supermarket on her way home from work. The family eats a lot of noodles, rice, meat, fish, and vegetables. They also like steak and sushi—raw fish served with rice and vegetables.

Junko buys most of her food at the supermarket.

After the evening meal, Emi goes out to another school. She is studying for special exams. She gets home at 10:00 P.M.

The subway train is the quickest way for Hajime to get to work.

13

# LIVING IN THE COUNTRY

The Yonezumi family outside their farmhouse. Seiji has already gone to work.

## THE YONEZUMI FAMILY

Seiji and Mariko Yonezumi work on a small farm. They have three boys, Tomoaki, who is twelve, Matsataka, who is nine, and Naochika, who is six. The children's grandparents, Kiyo and Toshikazu, live with them.

## WORK ON THE FARM

The grandparents do most of the work on the farm. The farm does not earn enough for the family to live on, so Seiji and Mariko both go out to work.

The family eats their meal off a low table. They sit on the floor.

Kiyo working in the fields. She is wearing typical work clothes. These allow her to move easily, and the hat protects her from the sun.

## THE CHILDREN'S DAY

Tomoaki and Matsataka have to walk more than a mile to get to school. Tomoaki has to leave for school at 7:30 A.M. On Fridays he goes from one school to another school, to have extra classes. Naochika goes to a nursery school.

The children like to watch TV and play games on their computer. They also like playing soccer with the other children in the village.

A soccer ball makes the walk to school more fun for Tomoaki.

# JAPANESE STORES

## DAILY SHOPPING

Japan has small stores and local markets where people can buy food each day. Farmers bring fruit and vegetables to market, and people sell live fish, swimming in water tanks, so people know the fish are fresh.

More and more Japanese people buy food from supermarkets. More women work full-time, and have to shop on their way home. Supermarkets are quick and easy.

**Market stalls are a good place to buy fresh, local food, like these vegetables.**

Japan is famous for its electronic goods. Most Japanese homes have computers, washing machines, TVs, and stoves.

## CITY SHOPPING

Japanese cities have many stores selling electronic **goods** and other expensive things, like clothes. People buy attractive things to wear for work. Young people like to wear jeans. Japanese people only wear traditional clothes on special occasions.

*Kimonos are traditional Japanese dresses. They cost a lot because they are made by hand. They take about 20 minutes to put on!*

# MADE IN JAPAN

Japan sells all sorts of **goods** to other countries, especially electronic goods. Goods that are sold to other countries are called exports.

## FACTORIES

Japanese factories make cars and motorcycles. They make electronic goods like computers, TVs, videos, CD players, cameras, watches, and calculators.

**Factories make a lot of smoke. This causes air pollution in nearby cities.**

# WORKERS

Japanese companies expect workers to work hard. Many workers stay with the same company for all their working lives. It is like a family. The company helps them to buy a home, makes sure they are looked after if they are sick, and even helps with the children's education. This encourages everyone to work together as part of the company team.

Now this is changing. Many younger workers move about much more, looking for better jobs and more pay.

*More cars are made in Japan than in any other country in the world.*

**Many Japanese car factories use robots to put the cars together. People check the work at the end.**

# SPORTS AND VACATIONS

**A sumo wrestling match. The best wrestlers in Japan are treated like movie stars.**

## SPORTS

One of the most famous Japanese sports is sumo wrestling. Sumo wrestlers try to throw each other out of a ring.

Other popular sports are **martial arts**, like judo and kendo. Baseball, soccer, swimming, and basketball are also popular. So is golf, but there are not many golf courses because there is not enough land to build them on.

People like to visit local parks. They are full of cherry blossoms in the spring.

## TIME OFF

Traditional Japanese hobbies include origami—making folded paper shapes—and flower arranging. Young people prefer karaoke (singing to a music tape) and playing computer games. People also visit religious shrines and enjoy walking in parks and flower gardens.

## VACATIONS

Many people come from all over the world to visit Japan. They visit the busy cities, the religious shrines, and Mount Fuji. Many Japanese people go to other countries for their vacations.

*The 1998 Winter Olympics will be held in Japan. There is a lot of snow in the mountains in the winter.*

# FESTIVALS AND CUSTOMS

## SPECIAL DAYS

There are many days off for special occasions in Japan. These include days when children or old people are given special treats, and the **emperor's** birthday. There are also New Year celebrations that go on for three days.

## RELIGIOUS FESTIVALS

Japan has two main religions, Shintoism (where nature and ancestors are important) and Buddhism (where people follow the teachings of the Buddha). Both religions have many festivals.

**At this winter festival in Osaka, men show how brave they are by not wearing clothes!**

These women are making tea in a special **ceremony**. It can take four hours to make!

# CUSTOMS

Many Japanese traditions are still important today. People like to watch Noh plays, which describe old battles and heroes. The actors wear costumes and masks that have looked the same for hundreds of years. Haiku is an old way of writing poetry. The poems have only three lines. Japanese people also enjoy new things, like computer games or rock music.

# JAPAN FACT FILE

## People

People from Japan are called Japanese.

## Capital city

The capital city of Japan is Tokyo.

## Largest cities

Tokyo is the largest city with nearly 12 million people. The second largest city is Yokohama. Osaka is the third largest city.

## Head of country

Japan has an **emperor** but it is ruled by a **government**.

## Population

There are 125 million people living in Japan.

## Money

Money in Japan is called the yen.

## Language

People speak Japanese. The language is written from top to bottom and left to right.

## Religion

Nearly all Japanese people belong to the Shinto or the Buddhist religion.

## MORE BOOKS TO READ

Doran, Clare. *The Japanese*. New York: Thomson Learning, 1995.
Kalman, Bobbie. *Japan, the People*. New York: Crabtree, 1989.

# GLOSSARY

**atomic bomb** This is a very powerful bomb that destroys people and buildings and also affects the air, making people sick long after it has exploded.

**capital city** This is the city in a country where the government is based.

**ceremony** This is an organized and formal way of doing things, often for religions or public occasions.

**coast** This is where the land meets the sea.

**emperor** The emperor of Japan used to rule the country and make all the decisions. Now there is a government chosen by the Japanese people. The emperor is still head of the country, but does not have any real power.

**fertilizer** This is a chemical mixture used as a plant food.

**government** These are the people who run a country.

**goods** These are the things people make.

**island** This is a piece of land with water all around it.

**lava** This is melted rock from under the Earth's surface.

**martial art** This is a type of sport, like fighting.

**pollution** This is dirt in the air, water, or on land.

**typhoons** These are violent storms with strong winds and rains.

**volcano** This is a mountain that sometimes throws out ash or melted rock.

# INDEX